An Altitude KIDS OWN NatureBook

W9-ATH-378

Baby Wild Animals

PUBLICATION INFORMATION

10, 9, 8, 7

We acknowledge the financial support of the
Government of Canada through the
Book Publishing Industry Development Program (BPIDP)
for our publishing activities.

Canadian Cataloguing in Publication Data
Schmidt, Dennis, 1921-
Kids own nature guide
(Kids own guides)
ISBN 1-55153-813-X
1. Animals--Infancy--Juvenile literature. I. Schmidt, Esther,
1922- II. Title. III. Series.
QL49.S35 1995   j591.3'9   C95-910301-5

Altitude GreenTree Program
Altitude will plant, in Canada, twice as many trees as were used in the manufacture
of this book. Altitude Publishing created this unique program in 1993.

Printed and bound in Canada by Friesen Printers

Altitude Publishing
1500 Railway Ave., Canmore, Alberta T1W 1P6
Order desk: 1-800-957-6888 • (403) 678-6888 • fax (403) 678-6951

BABY WILD ANIMALS

Photographs by Dennis and Esther Schmidt

Baby animals are as different as can be. Baby moose are awkward and ungainly. Baby bear cubs are playful. Bobcat kittens look very much like domestic kittens – but they certainly grow up to be very different.

One of the first steps in knowing more about the family life of wild animals is to know what the animals, both young and old, look like. This book will help you identify baby animals–because you just never know when you might see one next time you are out hiking.

Chipping Sparrow

Whitetailed Fawn

Cougar Kitten

Baby Ground Squirrels

Swan Cygnets

Merlin Chicks

Coyote Pup

Bighorn Lambs

Cougar Kitten

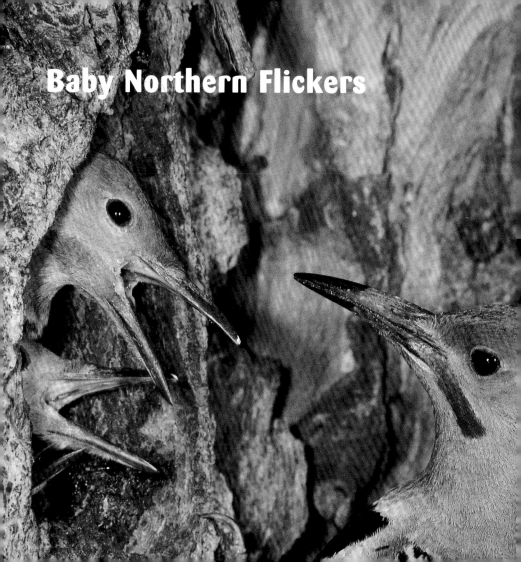

Baby Northern Flickers

Cedar Waxwing Nestlings

Elk Calf

Avocet Chicks

Saw Whet Owlet

Osprey Chicks

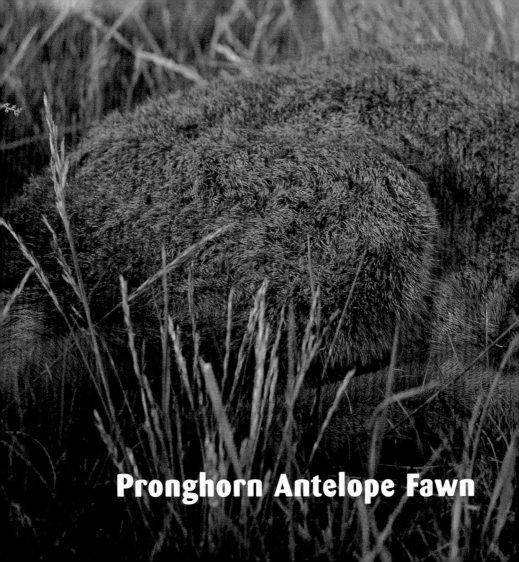

Pronghorn Antelope Fawn

Baby Rabbit

Prairie Dog Pup

Moose Calf

Baby Hummingbirds

Baby
Woodpeckers

Wolf Pups

Canada Goose Gosling

Black Bear Cubs

Mountain Goat Kid

Mule Deer Fawn

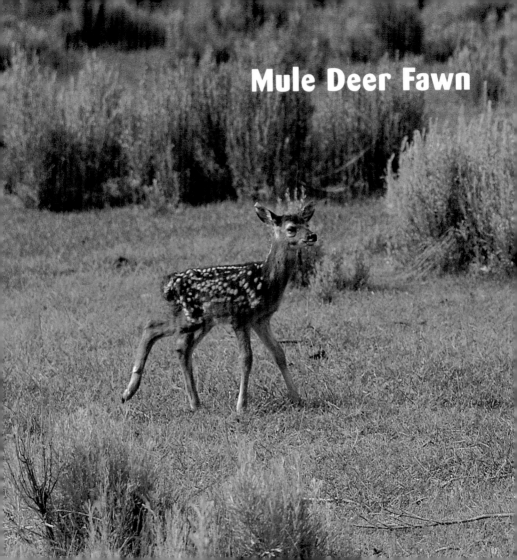

Mule Deer Fawn

Bighorn Lambs

Bighorn Lamb

Elk Calf

Loggerhead Shrike Nestlings

Bobcat Kittens

Black Bear Cubs

Red Fox Kits